A
Short Historical Sketch

on

Tapestry and Embroidery

by

J. Getz

Published for the benefit of
The Art Loan Exhibition
held April, 1895

New York

Copyright, 1895, by J. Getz.

In the interest of creating a more extensive selection of rare historical book reprints, we have chosen to reproduce this title even though it may possibly have occasional imperfections such as missing and blurred pages, missing text, poor pictures, markings, dark backgrounds and other reproduction issues beyond our control. Because this work is culturally important, we have made it available as a part of our commitment to protecting, preserving and promoting the world's literature. Thank you for your understanding.

INTRODUCTION.

E shall limit ourselves to the scope which these few pages afford as an introductory, and briefly outline the progress of Decorative Art, beginning with the Roman Empire, when Rome, under Nero and Trojan, set the example of an excessive love for ornament applied to all the useful arts, which was imitated throughout the East and West.

At the transference by Constantine to Byzantium, in the fourth century, a still greater degree of luxury was developed in the Eastern Empire, where the minute and overladen ornament, so affected by Orientals, was blended with the more artistic system of the West. Whilst this development of style was being formed, and was daily extending in the East, a change of a very different nature occurred in the West. The withdrawal of Roman legions from Germany, France and England, in the fifth century, deprived the people of those countries of the models, and in a great measure, of the means for effecting ornamental display.

The luxury of decoration was confined to royalty and to some of the powerful families, and it was duly displayed on certain occasions. War, and the hard struggle for existence were the main objects of all men's efforts, and the hands which in other times might peacefully guide the loom or shape the ductile metal into forms of beauty, grasped the sword, or were hard and horny with the roughest work of a slavish existence.

The decorative arts during this period and up to the eleventh century found a home in Byzantium, and radiated thence as from a center with increasing power. It was there that the most elaborate works in wood, ivory, metal and in textile art, were continually produced; being exported throughout Europe and parts of Asia, served as models which native artists imitated or were inspired by. During this period, the Church pressed into its service, with far-seeing wisdom, all that was best in the arts; architecture, sculpture, painting, music, rich costumes and the decorative arts generally.

A great impulse was given in the eleventh century to all branches of decorative art, by the advancing influence of the Normans in Europe, and although it was mainly through their connection with Greeks and Arabs in Sicily and Southern Italy that they obtained the means of putting into form their natural love of show and splendor, yet the innate and original genius of their race appears to have been so potent in guiding and directing the instruments at hand, that we may date from this time forward the commencement of a European style of decorative art, in contradistinction to that of Byzantium, which had up to this time, with few exceptions and modifications, been paramount.

By the twelfth century, or commencement of the thirteenth, the Roman-Persian foliage, the interlaced ribbon work, the jewels and beads of Byzantium were nearly out of vogue. The artist turned to Nature for aid and instruction, and there arose a school which might claim comparison, and in many respects outshone those of the ancient Greeks and Romans. "Fresh from the depressing bondage of a formal conventionality, these restorers of art must have felt a blind man's delight, whose eyes were suddenly opened, and who looked forth on a wonderful world, in which the meanest objects presented to the charmed gaze some features of beauty, and served to excite their newly aroused sense of the art of the Creator."

At this period, Nature was copied with truth, fidelity and spirit, but this would not have sufficed alone to have given ornamental art the charm it possessed, had it not been combined with conventional forms, and its merit was enhanced by a judicious combination of architectural features, such as mouldings and tracery, besides heraldic shields and figures.

During the fourteenth century, this progress was marked, so that we meet with tapestries, stained glass, carpets, rich furniture and costly utensils for the table—to be common in the castles of the noble and the wealthy.

In the fifteenth century, domestic architecture and furniture, of which it is more or less a reflex, became of a highly ornamental nature, and the homes of the nobles and rich merchants were made interesting with rich furniture and minor accessories. The illustrations and the illuminated manuscripts of this century, bear out faithfully for out study many examples. We may note the rich bed hangings, curtains, leaded glass, carved furniture, candlesticks, stone chimney-pieces, wall tapestries, carpets and jewelry, in the descriptions of great mansions and palaces still preserved in France, Italy and England.

The splendor of living was greatly affected during the fifteenth century, by the great Dukes of Burgundy and Brabant; after this period, when the Gothic monumental art was being gradually lost, in the swift decline of that architecture to which it had lent and still furnished so powerful a charm, another school arose in Central Italy, in which nature and the models of antiquity were at first so nearly blended, that it is difficult to assign a preponderance to either. To the genius, taste and patience of Michael Angelo, Lorenzo Ghiberti, Verocchio, and Lucca della Robbia, is due the credit of having perfected a style founded on those inspirations, and their masterpieces are not only the glory of Renaissance art, but the masterpieces of all existing works founded on this school.

Shortly after the school of nature was thus illustrated by its masters, and whilst the ornament of the Cisalpine schools was dying out in glory, different but scarcely inferior to that of the most prosperous age, the revival of the antique was carrying all before it, and the artists of the age bowed down in enthusiastic worship before the unveiled genius of ancient Rome. This result, however, was not consummated in a few years, and the intervening period is characterized by a style of ornament in which Nature and the Cisalpine schools only gradually gave way to the introduction of the classic models.

Up to the first years of the sixteenth century, Nature still lent a great charm to the decorative arts. Italy was irradiated with its dying emanations, and the race of smaller masters in Germany, the Netherlands and France continued more or less throughout this century to sustain its existence by numerous and graceful productions.

By the close of the sixteenth century, however, the antique reigned supreme, and Italy set the fashion to all Europe, where the greatest artists did not disdain to exercise their genius on the commonest requirements of every-day life. Noble palaces, which demanded fitting ornaments, rose throughout Italy and Spain, and England, too, had her share of fine mansions.

The internal decoration of a palace in this and the succeeding century, is now familiar to us all; in France, England and Flanders, the panelled walls, the magnificent wood and stone mantels, the finely designed stucco ceiling, the stained glass windows, the rich hangings; whilst in Italy the walls were resplendent with frescoes by great masters, and the ceilings and cornices were one mass of color and gilding; accessories in fitting such splendor were not wanting. Venice contributed rare works in glass and furniture; Arras, Fontainbleu and Brussels sent forth tapestries; Milan, Nurenburg and Augsburg produced splendid examples of ornamental sculpture in metal and wood, ivory and stone; Flanders, Germany and Switzerland the best stained and painted glass; Limoges the most beautiful enamels; Florence the finest bronzes and works in mosaics; Central Italy its boldly colored iridescent and glittering earthen ware, and China some of its marvelous porcelain.

Luxury may now be fairly said to have become common amongst the wealthier classes; many of these productions were purchased as much for show as for use. Great value was attached to them—as may be gathered from the inventories of the times. It is not without reason that store was set on articles of this nature, for the greatest artists employed their talents upon them; thus we find that the fine vestments still preserved in the sacristy of San Giovanni, at Florence, were designed by Antonio Pollaiuolo, and were executed by Paolo de Verona with the needle, a work requiring twenty-six years of labor.

Giuliano and Benedetto da Maiano were unrivalled in carved and inlaid furniture; the Florentine painter, Dello, celebrated for his paintings on marriage chests; Guiliano d'Agnolo and his brothers were particularly renowned for their carved work; Bacchhiacca designed embroidery for bed hangings, with figure subjects, which were unfinished at his death and continued under the direction of Vasari. Perino del Vaga appears to have been driven in his labors for designs of embroideries, carving, and other things ornamental, by the capricious Farnese, and other signori. He was always surrounded by a crowd of painters, sculptors, masters in stucco, carvers of wood, gilders, embroiderers, and, in fact, artists and workers of every kind, by whom his mind was kept in perpetual turmoil for designs.

Guilio Romano made designs for tapestry and cloth of Arrazzi, Raffael's cartoons for similar work so famous and often referred to by all writers on tapestries, the carvers, Carota Andrea de Cosimo and Andrea del Sarto, who are referred to by Vasari. Girolamo Gengaa modelled in wax certain drinking vessels to be executed in silver for the Bishop of Sinigaglio, and others for the Duke Francesco Maria, of Urbino, whilst Cellini, the great master, produced his marvels in precious metals. Nor was it in Italy alone that the great artists of this and the succeeding century turned their attention to the decorative arts, in the names of Duerer, Vischer, Holbein, Lucan Von Leyden, Gonjon, and a host of others only less celebrated are intimately connected with the development and practice of the ornamental art.

After the middle of the seventeenth century, another great change was effected in decorative art by the means of an educational establishment founded by Louis XIV. at the Gobelins, where not only tapestry alone, but furniture and metal work, gold and silver work was manufactured to form something new, tired of the quiet system of antique art, yet neglecting to take advantage of nature for its model, this school fell from bad to worse. It is unnecessary to follow the wanderings and errors of declining art during the eighteenth century. Three or four methods of decoration, particularly mark the foregoing epoch. The varnished coloring of furniture of every kind, with painted flowers and figure subjects, of Martin; the metal and wood inlay by Boule, and the use of porcelain and lacquer panels, etc. An affectation of rich and fantastic decoration, however, poorly compensated for the loss of all that is valuable and noble in art, and it was no doubt with a feeling of mental relief that people returned at the close of the eighteenth century to the purity and simplicity of the lately studied remains of ancient Greece and Rome.

It must ever be, that by studying all past art, returning then to nature with attentive eye and appreciative spirit, and make use of those models, perfect or suggestive which lie scattered so profusely around us—thus the true artist, by virtue of his nature, is inspired to create for our enjoyment and use, lasting treasures, such as may be collected in other centuries yet to come.

We owe a debt of gratitude to the antiquaries of

the seventeenth and eighteenth centuries, when the desire for such knowledge gradually increased, when archæology began to assume the form of method of a science, which threw its light, dim, indeed, at first, not only on the long-past days of ancient Greece and Rome, but in the yet more remote gloom of Egypt, the obscurity of early European life was quickly dissolving under the light of these periods. When such researches were recognized as of the highest importance not only to art, but to the general advancement and certitude of all historic knowledge. At present this peculiarly the case; for we live at a time when there is an almost universal desire to preserve whatever may tend to elucidate the entire history of the human race.

BRUSSELS TAPESTRY—SILK AND GOLD POINT.

ALTAR FRONT—EMBROIDERY.

TAPESTRY.

"AMONG the monuments that the past has bequeathed to us, there are none which offer so much material for the archæologist as ancient tapestries. The vicissitudes of this industry are closely connected with the history of the countries in which it is practiced, and not only does the greater part of these productions bear the imprint of the epoch in which they are produced, but we find in them the reflections of the beliefs and of the great events of their time, with all the details of its architecture and its costumes. They give us in fact, a picture of the intimate life of each country."
—*M. Castel, Les Tapisseries.*

Tapestry is neither real weaving nor true embroidery, but in a manner unites in its working these processes into one. Though wrought in a loom and upon a warp stretched out along its frame, it has no woof thrown across those threads with a shuttle or any like appliance, but, its weft is done with many threads, all variously colored and intertwined by hand from the spool or "flute" upon a series of closely set white strings or "chains" of worsted or wool, thus forming a web and producing combinations of lines and tints analogous to those obtained by the painter with his brush.

M. E. Müntz, in *La Tapisseries*, writes that "Tapestry differs from embroidery in this, that in it the pictures produced are an integral part of the texture, while in the latter they are simply superimposed on a tissue already existing. It also differs from woven fabrics by being always the work of the hand and not an unlimited mechanical repetition of the same design, so that each piece produced is distinctly original."

The Rev. Dr. Daniel Rock, in "*Textile Fabrics*," referring to the probable age of this art, says that, "From the way tapestry is spoken of in the Holy Writ, we may be sure that the art is very old, and if it did not take its rise in Egypt we are led to conclude that it soon became successfully cultivated by the people of that land. The woman in the Book of Proverbs says: 'I have woven my bed with cords, I have covered it with painted tapestry brought from Egypt.' We find, therefore, that it was not only employed as an article of household furniture among the Israelites, but that the Egyptians were the makers."

From Egypt through Western Asia the art of tapestry-making found its way to Europe, and was successfully followed in many parts of France, Flanders, Germany, England, Italy and Spain.

The history of tapestry from the Middle Ages onward is that of painting, for at that epoch the style is that of the illuminator and the painters of glass. Among the other manual labors, followed in religious houses, this handicraft was one, and monks became some of the best workmen; the altars and walls of their churches were hung with tapestry, secular trade guilds were formed in towns of France and ancient Flanders, and several of these places won especial fame, but Arras outran them all, so that "Arras-work," "Arras-hangings" or "Arrazzi" came to be a common word. meaning all sorts of tapestry woven by hand. It is but one among other terms by which, during the Middle Ages, tapestry was called wherever it was made, for during the 14th and 15th centuries, Arras was the city from whence came the most important tapestries. They stood for all that was richest in color, choicest in material and the finest production of the tapestry weaver. Their reputation had penetrated even to the Orient. Its earliest name was "Saracenic work" (Opus Saracenicum).

The earliest tapestries of the Middle Ages still

in existence are German, probably of the 12th century, notably that in the Church of Saint Géréon at Cologne, which is Byzantine in style, and fragments of which may be seen at the Germanic Museum of Nuremberg, the South Kensington Museum in London, and the Industrial Museum, Lyons. Others are in the churches of Halberstadt and Quedlinburg, attributed to the end of the 12th century.

At first, tapestry was woven, or wrought, as in the East, on a low or horizontal loom. The artisans of France and Flanders were the first to introduce the upright or vertical frame known as "Haute lisse," in contradistinction to the low or horizontal frame called "Basse lisse." With the upright, as with the flat loom, the workman gropes a great deal in the dark over his work. In both, he is obliged to put in the threads on the back or wrong side of the piece, following the sketch as best he can behind the white strings or chains of the warp. In the flat or horizontal frame, the face is downward, and much less easy to observe and correct any fault, while in the upright or vertical frame, as used, for example, at the Gobelin works, the weaver may go in front and study his own work, in open view on one hand, and the original design on the other, he can rapidly amend as he goes on, step by step, the smallest error, if but a single

MORTLAKE TAPESTRY

thread. One can scarcely particularize the superiority of one loom over the other; only when put side by side and finished, may the difference be noted.

In his study upon decorative art, M. Chas. M. Blanc says: "Our ancestors of the Middle Ages lived in a more poetic and attractive age than ours. They were poets in their architecture, full of religious and chivalric sentiment; they were poets in their glass paintings, by intercepting the light to shine resplendent with a paradise of color; they were poets in their tapestry with which they covered their walls, and which they used as enclosures when they divided their walls or chambers into small alcoves. These tapestries enveloped them in mystery. *Intrigues d'amour!* State secrets, conspiracies, surprises, hidden passages—all these in time of chivalry, of war, of stratagem, were in turn concealed and disclosed by such hangings which covered the walls, and the fringes of which trailed upon the floor." Tapestry is said to have been introduced in France as hangings for walls as early as the 9th century; and in the year 1205, there was a manufactory of such hangings at Poitiers.

In 1477, Louis XI. conquered Arras and obliged all the tapestry weavers to quit their looms, and this date marks the fall of the industry in that city.

Brussels, Audenarde, Lille, Bruges, Tournai, Valencienes, Paris, Fountainbleau, Florence, etc., were also centers of tapestry weaving in this century, but the leading city of the 16th century was Brussels. "No time and no country presented anything comparable with the prosperity of the Brussels tapestry weavers during this period. Henceforth, tapestry is everywhere appreciated, everywhere in demand; from this moment, the Ateliers of Brussels were proclaimed to be the first in Christendon; all the princes in Europe hastened to demand replicas of these famous hangings."
—*M. Guiffrey, Histories de la Tapisseries.*

The 16th century is often referred to as the "Golden Age of Tapestry," and examples of this period, though hardly numerous, may be seen in some of our private collections of to-day, and in the Museums and Cathedrals of Europe.

The productions of this period by the Flemish masters may be best studied at Madrid; the Musée des Gobelins possesses some fine examples, the Louvre, the South Kensington Museum at London, and also our museums.

The culminating point in the history of tapestry was unquestionably the employment of the genius of Raphael at the instance of Leo X. to make the cartoons from which were executed a series of pictures from the New Testament, "The Acts of

ATTAR FRONT—RENAISSANCE EMBROIDERY.

GOBELIN TAPESTRY—CALIDONIAN BOAR HUNT.

the Apostles," for the adornment of the walls of the Sistine Chapel. These cartoons of Raphael were sent to Brussels by Pope Leo X. in 1515, and the tapestries were received at Rome four years later with universal admiration. The cartoons were also later used by the Mortlake factory in England, and the Gobelin factory in France, a suite from each are now in the Garde Meuble, Paris. The Mortlake factory was established by James I. in 1603, and was continued with much zeal under Charles I., who lavished large sums for its maintenance.

At the manufactory founded by Francis I. at Fontainebleau, Flemish workmen were employed. This establishment was kept up by his successor, Henry II., and in the year 1597, Henry IV. is said to have reëstablished a manufactory of tapestry on the premises of the Gobelins, in the Faubourg Saint-Marcel.

"Towards the middle of the 15th century, Jehan Gobelin from Reims, founded upon the borders of the River Bièvre, a dye-house which became celebrated and brought to its proprietors a fortune, due to the quality of the products emanating from its vats; a quality due to the skill of its dyers and not to the waters of the Bièvre, which never had any particular dyeing qualities. The Gobelin family carried on this industry even as late as about 1655, and by singular favor of destiny, by the simple fact of the installation of skillful tapestry weavers in this ancient property, they acquired immortality without even having woven a single yard of tapestry,"—*M. Gerspach, la Manufacture Nationale des Gobolins.*

The Royal manufacturing of Gobelins was founded by Louis XIV., in 1662. Colbert was appointed its first superintendent, and to him was confided its administration. The management of the ateliers devolved upon Charles Le Brun. "The sentiment of decoration is so strong in him that his paintings are transfigured in passing from the canvas to the warp; their translation into a different art gives them more *éclat*, a richer and stronger harmony."—*M. Guiffrey, Historie de la Tapisserie.*

The Royal manufactory of Beauvais was also established at this period by Louis XIV. with Louis Huiard of Paris at its head. The atelier received a great impetus in 1684, by the appointment of Phillipe Nehagle of Audenrade as director, and later by Oudry (1734), who also filled the same function for the Gobelins. These two men largely contributed in making Beauvais the most important atelier in France after the Gobelins.

In the 18th century, the renowned ateliers of the capitals of the low countries were in decadence.

The success of the manufacture of the Gobelins effaced their reputation. Henceforth, the name of Gobelin became, not only in France, but also in other countries, a synonym for tapestries of finished perfection. Florence, Rome, Berlin, Munich, Dresden, Madrid, and even Russia, contributed to the encouragement of this industry.

In the 19th century we have to record rather the failure than the success of tapestry weaving, if we omit the factories of Gobelins and Aubusson (Brussels, Munich, Rome, Windsor, have all been given up), and the adoption in our midst, on the Bronx River, of this ancient and interesting art.

EMBROIDERY.

THE art of working with the needle any fanciful design, upon webs woven of linen, cotton or silk is of the highest antiquity. Those patterns, after so many fashions, which we see figured upon the garments worn by men and women upon the Egyptian and Assyrian monuments, but especially in the burned clay vases made and painted by the Greeks in their earliest as well as their latest times, or which we read about in the writings of that people, were not wrought in the loom, but worked by the needle.

The art of embroidery appears to have been practiced in Assyria as early as in Egypt, and was not only carried to great perfection in that region, but was probably introduced from there to India.

It is ingeniously conjectured by Gottfried Semple (in an essay on the Four Elements of Architecture, 1852,) that the art of the Assyrian sculptor had its origin in the embroidered work of that country, and he refers to the peculiar interlacings, knots and similar patterns in Assyrian architecture in support of his opinion. The costumes of the Kings, priests and warriors, so vividly represented in sculptures now brought to light, afford abundant evidence of the extent to which this kind of ornamentation was carried in Assyria.

Our first distinct notice of embroidery occurs in reference to the erection of the Tabernacle in the Wilderness, and we are expressly told that Moses was "skilled in all the learning of the Egyptians."

Martial adds that the art of embroidery was commonly practiced in Egypt, and the Hebrews, on leaving the country of their captivity, took advantage of the knowledge they had acquired to make the rich hangings and fabrics described by Moses. And Martial also compares the woven fabrics of Egypt with the "embroidered" work of Babylon.

It is clear from Homer that the Grecian ladies were skilled and industrious in the use of the needle. On the departure of Ulysses for Ilium, Penelope is described as throwing over him an upper garment, embroidered on gold, on which were represented the incidents of the chase.

Pliny says that the Phrygians invented embroidery, and that garments so ornamented were called Phrygionic; hence, an embroider was called in

Latin "Phrygio," and needle work "Phrygium" or "Phrygian work." When the design was wrought in solid gold (as often happened), with wire or golden threads, the embroidery so worked was called Auriphrygium. From this term comes the English word "Orphrey." While Phrygia in general, and Babylon in particular (as Pliny also tells us), became celebrated for the beauty of its embroidery. The Assyrians adorned their robes lavishly with needle work for which one of their cities was famous, for the reputation which Babylon had won for her textiles and needle-work, still lived up to the first century of our era.

The paintings and mosaics of Herculaneum and Pompeii, furnished numerous illustrations of costumes, from which it is evident that in the prosperity of those cities the art under consideration was practiced with great taste and ability. It was, however, under the patronage of the Emperor Constantine that embroidery was brought to the high degree of perfection which it attained in ancient times, and which indeed has since been scarcely surpassed.

M. Digby Wyatt (Industrial Arts of 19th Century, 1852,) refers to the encouragement which embroidery received from the taste of barbaric splendor and personal adornment in which the founder of the Greek Empire so largely indulged. He states that "in the earliest diptychs we find indications of embroidery in portions of garments represented in consular portraits. The most ancient manuscripts and mosaics afford still clearer evidence as to the early developed partiality of the Greeks for similar rich decorations. Their intercourse with Persia and the East no doubt fostered this taste, and since the inhabitants of those regions had long been famed for the magnificence of their costumes and the skill with which their precious cloth and hangings were executed in the loom and adorned by the needle, it is reasonable, therefore, to find in the earliest representation of Greek embroidery an ornamental character. In proportion as the Saracenic races increased, so do we more and more clearly recognize the influence of the arts of design which they practiced, re-acting upon the Byzantines, from whom the first and leading elements of these arts had been derived."

Embroidery is perhaps one of the most favorite of all the fine arts, since it alone was practiced by the ladies of the very highest class in all ages. The retired life of the cloister and the chateau did not alone contribute towards its practice, but also the busy court life; and it is recorded that even Marie de Medici in the moments of her leisure, amid politics, found time and pleasure in her embroidery work.

DALMATIC GOLD EMBROIDERY—XVI. CENTURY.

Women in the middle ages were so ready with the needle that they could make their embroidery look as if it had been done in the loom. The fashion for this art of embroidery was general among the high class during the middle ages and was counted highly among the possessions of every house.

The monks devoted themselves to the cultivation of letters, the illumination of manuscripts and other useful arts; whilst their pious sisters of the convent, and the noble dames whose lords were occupied abroad, solaced their solitude with the fabrication or decoration of church furniture, and the vestments of priests, the robes of state of monarchs and nobles, and the surcoats of warriors.

Towards the latter end of the 13th century, embroidery obtained for its several styles and various sorts of ornamentation a distinguishing and technical nomenclature. "Opus plumarium" was the usual term for what is now called embroidery, and was given to needlework of this kind, because the stitches were laid down long-wise and not across (over-lapping one another like the feathers in the plumage of a bird), and aptly called feather stitch. The Opus Pulvinarium, or "cushion style" was like the modern so-called Berlin work. The Opus Pectineum was a kind of woven work imitation of embroidery and employed to supply it.

A stitch differing from any of these was invented in England near the end of the 13th century, and termed Opus Anglicum, which was very beautiful and novel. It consisted of a method of mixing the feather stitch with a style of needlework and mechanism, long a puzzle among archæological writers; but if we examine this work we find that it is a sort of chain-stitch, and the feather-stitch, while the newly practiced mechanical appliance was brought into use in the whole embroidery. With a little thin iron rod ending in a small bulb or smooth knob, heated properly, those spots in circular and straight lines were pressed down. By the hollows thus lastingly sunk, a play of light and shadows was brought out which at a very short distance lends to the portion so treated low relief, although not merely the faces and extremities, but the dresses, also, of the persons figured were generally wrought in chain-stitch and afterwards treated as described.

The style of raised embroidery, gained great reputation and was practiced largely during the latter end of the Middle Ages, and especially in Italy and England during the 17th century. Few people of the present century have any idea of the labor, the money and the length of time often bestowed upon embroidery. In the life of Antonio

HIGH WARP LOOM.

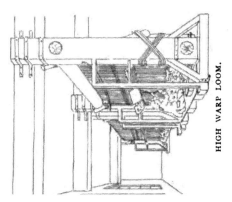

LOW WARP LOOM.

Pollainolo, by Vasari, a vestment is mentioned which took twenty-six years for its completion.

The *opus consutum* or cut-work, called in France *appliqué*, is a term of rather wide meaning, as it takes in several sorts of decorative accompaniments to needle-work.

How highly embroideries were appreciated and coveted, we may find in many old documents, and the discriminating accuracy with which old writers noted the several kinds of textile gifts bestowed upon churches or persons of state, is as instructive as praiseworthy.

CPSIA information can be obtained
at www.ICGtesting.com
Printed in the USA
BVHW011155050822
643696BV00006B/70